Trust Me, I'm a Doctor

A visual catalog of
generic Dr Pepper-style
soft drink logos,
1995-2020

A Birchwood Palace publication
BP009

Visit us on the World Wide Web at
birchwoodpalace.com

Compiled by Andy Sturdevant

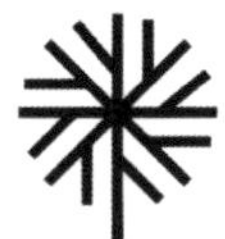

Birchwood Palace Industries, L.L.C. is a publisher of artists
books, zines and other small-run printed materials. It is a project
of Andy Sturdevant, and is based in Minneapolis, Minnesota.

Introduction

There is no such person as Dr. Pepper, or at least no such person recognized by the United States government. Sure, there are persistent legends of a Dr. Charles Pepper of Virginia, mentor to pharmacy proprietor Charles Morrison of Waco, Texas, in whose pharmacy the soft drink was first formulated in 1885. Morrison was said to have named the drink in Dr. Pepper's honor, or perhaps in honor of Dr. Pepper's daughter Ruth, a long-lost love. In the trademark filing for the soft drink, however, the company is clear that it's a "fanciful" name – that is, named for no such person, living or dead. There is no Dr. Pepper. The question of the identity of Dr Pepper, both the historic figure and the soft drink, is a persistent one.

Specifically, there is this question: what type of soft drink is Dr Pepper, exactly? This has always presented a challenge for marketers. How would you even describe the taste? "Peppery"? Kind of, but not really. "Like prune juice?" Well, that's rumored to be one of the twenty-three secret ingredients, though Dr Pepper says it isn't. Legally, it's not really even a "cola." In 1963, a federal court ruled that Dr Pepper, not being made with kola nuts, was not in fact a "cola product." This made it easier for independent bottlers to distribute Dr Pepper without violating exclusive territorial rights agreements with Coca-Cola and Pepsi, creating an opening for the drink to go from a regional curiosity to become the third most popular soft drink in the United States.

All of this ambiguity does make it tough to describe what it is, though. For a few years in the 1960s, Dr Pepper's tagline declared it was "America's most misunderstood soft drink." Mostly, people know a few things: it's in maroon packaging, it has "Doctor" in the name, and it tastes like...well, it tastes like Dr Pepper.

This makes the job of those marketing the many knock-offs tough, too. The "Dr." part is the primary calling card, a vestigial element of the drink's roots as a medicinal cure-all. More accurately, of course, it's not "Dr." but "Dr" in the case of Dr Pepper. The company decided in the 1950s the logo was easier to read without the period. (In this book, logos that also omit the period are marked with a ‡ symbol.)

Nearly every supermarket chain in America has its own in-house Dr Pepper alternative. This book collects the approaches those chains' designers took in branding their products so it was close enough to Dr Pepper to be recognizable to the consumer as a "Pepper drink" (whatever that might be), but different enough that it didn't invite a lawsuit. Typically, there are a few approaches:

The 'Sparkle' Approach: These emphasize the drink's sensory qualities. Dr Pepper-style drinks are more of an acquired taste than standard colas: not as sweet, hints of anise, licorice and plum, and a famously prickly aftertaste. Many names and visual identities suggest popping, fizziness, the bite of a cold soft drink on your tongue or the rush of the caffeine and all of those spices: Drs. Wow, Zing, Cool, Buzz, Sparkle, Smooth, Perky, Rush, Pop, and Fizz, for example. Taken together, in fact, those ten adjectives do give a rough sense for the sensory experience of drinking a Dr Pepper.

The 'Rocket' Approach: The caffeine content of Dr Pepper-style drinks isn't significantly greater than regular colas, and certainly not even close to Mountain Dew-style drinks. Still, the perception remains, so many of these drinks have fairly belligerent, bombastic names that suggest being smashed by caffeine and spices: Drs. Dynamite, Wham, Rocket, and Thunder.

The 'Since 1908' Approach: Introduced in 1885, Dr Pepper has Coca-Cola beat by a year, and Pepsi by a decade. Just the fact that "Doctor" is in the name more closely ties the product to soda pop's pharmacy counter roots. A common approach will be to suggest a historical-sounding figure, like Drs. Bob, Starr or Schnee, or use fonts and stylistic flourishes that suggest Americana (see examples 37, 41 and 47).

The 'Radical' Approach: Paradoxically, Dr Pepper is *also* sometimes perceived as a choice for youthful, individualistic tastemakers too weird for heritage brands like Coke and Pepsi. To that end, many of these logos – in the names, but especially in the graphics – draw on whatever signifiers of youth culture are present in the larger culture, which usually makes the packaging look absurdly outdated in a few

years. (Mountain Dew and energy drink knock-offs have this problem, too.) The most extreme example is the logo for Dr. Publix, representing the genteel Southern grocery chain, showing a wild-haired figure in a lab coat thrashing away at a rave. Turn of the millennium techno font treatments abound in examples 14, 38 and 53, as well as the use of slangy terms like Phizz and Radical.

On the topic of self-consciously offbeat turn of the millennium free-thinkers, Dr Pepper knockoffs have long been a fascination of the Internet. It's that amateur enthusiasm for finding and collecting as many cans of Dr Pepper knockoffs as possible that largely made this book possible. Subreddits, Wikis and Facebook pages devoted to the phenomenon still abound, but many of the sources for the digital illustrations in this book come from very old-school personal websites of the pre-social media era. The Highly Unofficial Dr Pepper FAQ, run by Christopher Flaherty and updated regularly from the late 1990s to 2012, contains the most comprehensive listing of this paleolithic lineup of Angelfire, Tripod and AOL tribute websites. You can find the FAQ page at freenewyork.net/dpfaq.html. The list of sites is toward the bottom in Section 2.4, and it's extensive. My personal favorite is The Not Very Authoritative Doctor Soda Page, hosted on an MIT server and (very obviously) not updated in twenty years. My gratitude and a hoisted bottle of Dr. Rocket to them all.

Andy Sturdevant
Summer 2022

Dr Pepper logomarks since 1971

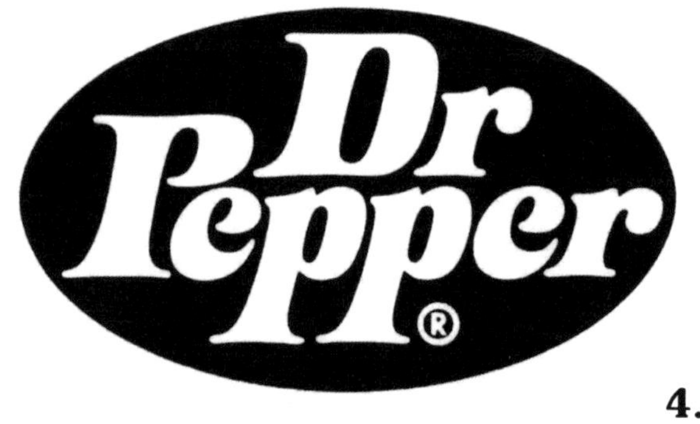

4.

5.

6.

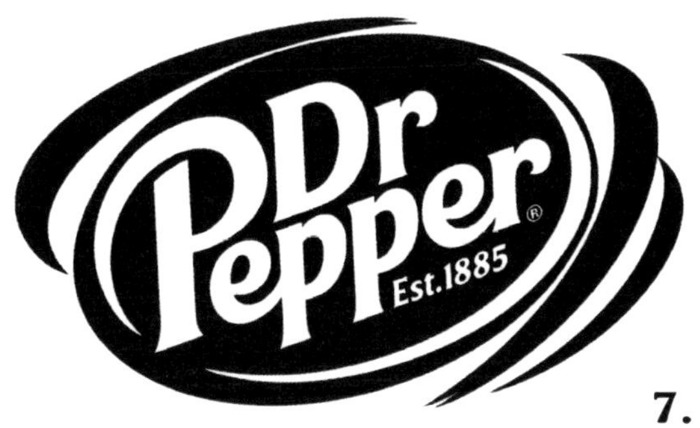

7.

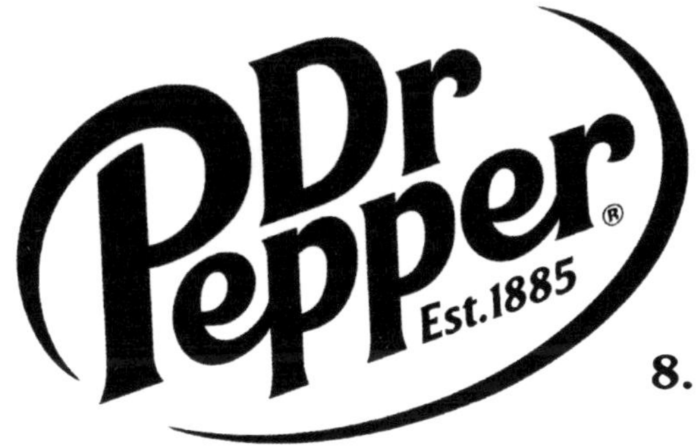

8.

4. **1971-1984**. The roll-out of this new logo in the early 1970s coincided with the first time Dr Pepper was marketed more aggressively to a national audience; prior to this, Dr Pepper was thought of as a strictly regional, Southern phenomenon, like RC Cola or Cheerwine. This logo dispensed with the kicky, thin serif typeface of earlier mid-century iterations, and has a chunky, hand-lettered quality that's both appropriately "old-timey" and in tune with the contemporary groovy aesthetic. Many Pepper imitators featured in this book use this logotype as a starting place, particularly examples 15-20. **5**. **1984-1997**. The logo pulls up at an action-oriented 60 degree angle, where it will stay for all subsequent iterations. **6**. **1997-2005**. With each new version, the chunky '70s serifs get leaner. **7**. **2005-2015**. "Est. 1885" added, if there were any doubt that among the dozens of imitators, this Dr is the genuine article. **8**. **2015-present**. A focus once again on the elliptical oval mark from 1971.

9. Dr. IGA, 2020. IGA Inc., Chicago, Ill. **10.** Dr. Pop, date unknown. Save-A-Lot Food Stores, Ltd., St. Ann, Mo. **11.** Dr. Bob, date unknown. Giant Food of Maryland, LLC, Landover, Md ‡ **12.** Dr. Wow, 2000. Shurfine International, Tigard, Ore. **13.** Dr Fizz, 2008. Tesco PLC, Welwyn Garden City, U.K. ‡ **14.** Dr. M, date unknown. Meiijer, Inc., Greenville, Mich.

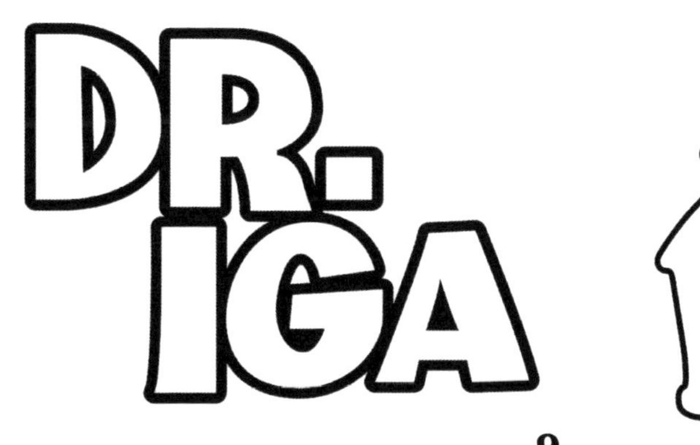

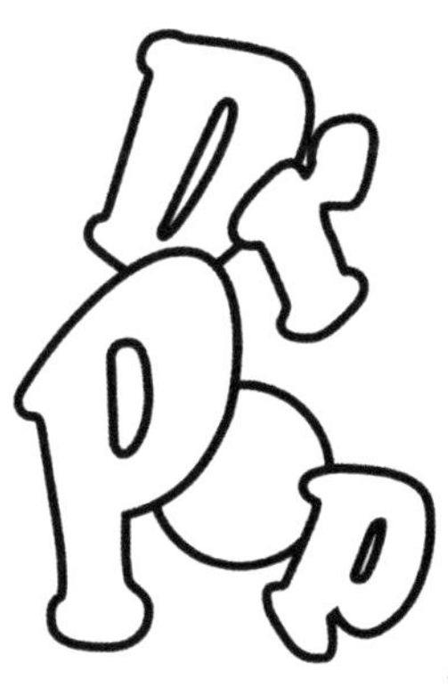

9. 10.

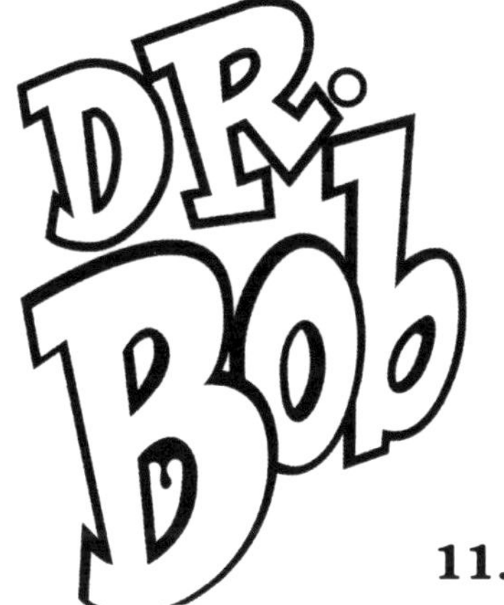

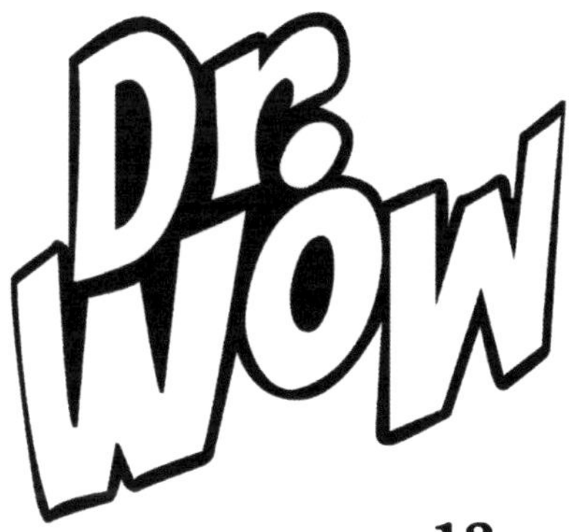

11. 12.

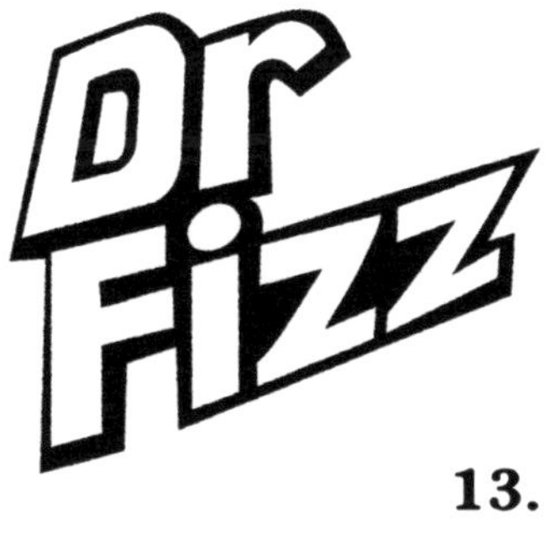

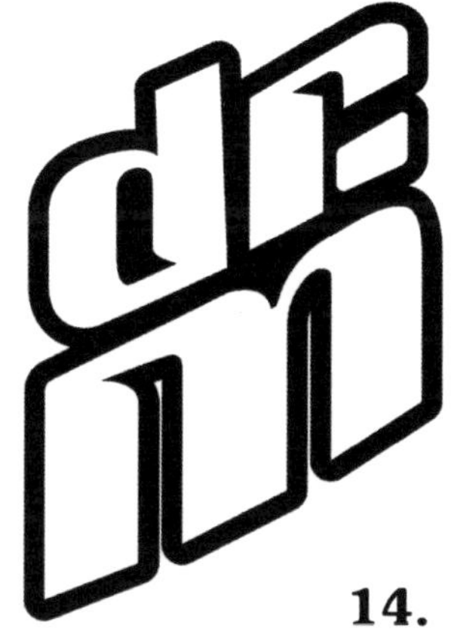

13. 14.

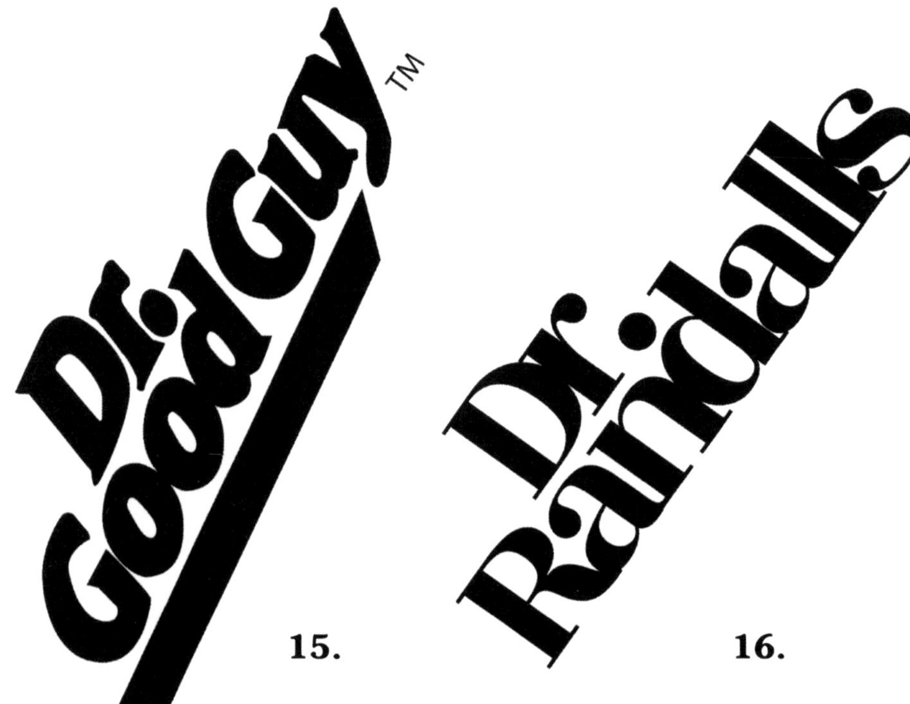

15.

16.

All chunky serifs here! **15.** Dr. Good Guy, 2002. Kalil Bottling Co., Tuscon, Ariz. The company motto is "The Good Guys at Kalil." **16.** Dr. Randalls, 2003. Randalls Food Markets, Houston, Tex. **17.** Dr A+, date unknown. Albertsons Companies, Inc., Boise, Idaho. ‡ **18**. Dr. Radical, early 2000s. Adirondack Beverages, Scotia, N.Y. Adirondack currently offers a range of "old-schools sodas" which sadly lacks a Dr Pepper variety. **19.** Dr. Skipper, late 2000s. Safeway, Inc., Pleasanton, Calif. **20**. Dr Perfect, early 2000s. BI-LO, Jacksonville, Fla. Drs Perfect have also been spotted at Giant Food stores in the mid-Atlantic by Internet soda pop aficionados, but it's unclear if it's the same brand. The BI-LO brand itself was eliminated by their parent company in 2021. ‡

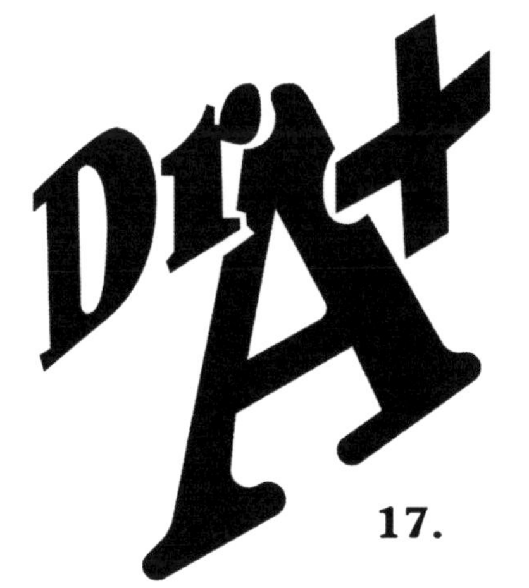

17.

Dr.Radical

18.

Dr.Skipper

19.

Dr Perfect

20.

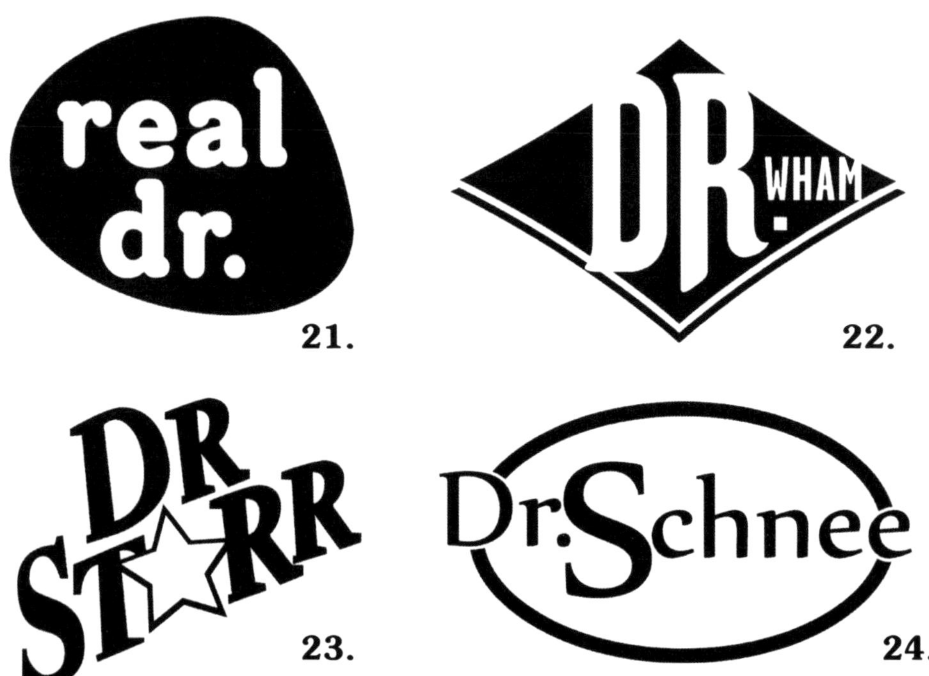

21. Real Dr., 2022. Sunny Select private label for Lucky Stores, San Leandro, Calif. **22**. Dr. Wham, 2022. Buffalo Rock Company, Birmingham, Ala. Buffalo Rock is an independent Pepsi bottler that sells Dr. Wham in Southern markets where the company doesn't have territorial rights to sell Dr Pepper. **23**. Dr Starr, date unknown. Lucky Stores, San Leandro, Calif. Dr Starr was replaced by the Real Dr. (see 16, and note period after Dr.). ‡ **24**. Dr. Schnee, date unknown. Vess Soda, St. Louis, Mo. Replaced by Dr. Vess (see example 55). ‡ **25**. Dr. Dazzle, 2019. Aldi U.S., Batavia, Ill. **26**. Dr. Dynamite, date unknown. Signature Select private label for Albertsons Companies, Inc., Boise, Idaho. **27**. Dr. Rush, date unknown. R.J. Corr Naturals, Posen, Ill. Corr brought a suit against Coca-Cola in 1997, alleging Surge soda's "Feed the Rush" slogan was a trademark infringement of Dr. Rush's slogan "The Rush is on." **28**. Dr. Cool, 1996. Cool Inc., Richardson, Tex. A short-ived Dallas-based independent manufacturer active in the mid-1990s. **29**. Dr. Nehi, c. 1972. Royal Crown Cola, Columbus, Ga. Nehi is one of the oldest soda brands in America. This groovy logo, designed by New York-based agency Gerstman & Meyers, was introduced in 1972. In fact, RC Cola is today owned by...Keurig Dr Pepper.

Dr. Dazzle

25.

Dr. Dynamite

26.

Dr. Rush

27.

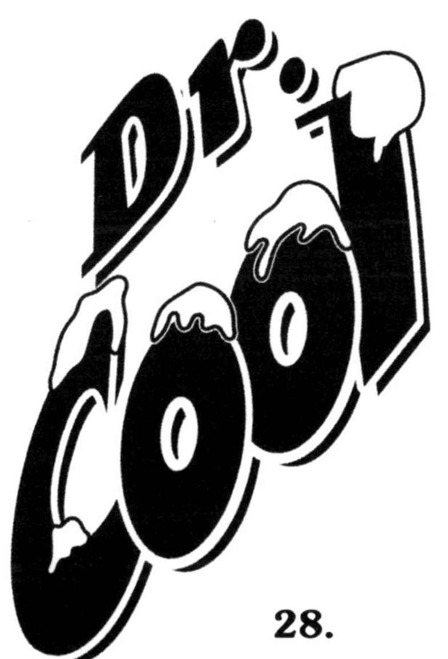

28.

Dr. Nehi

29.

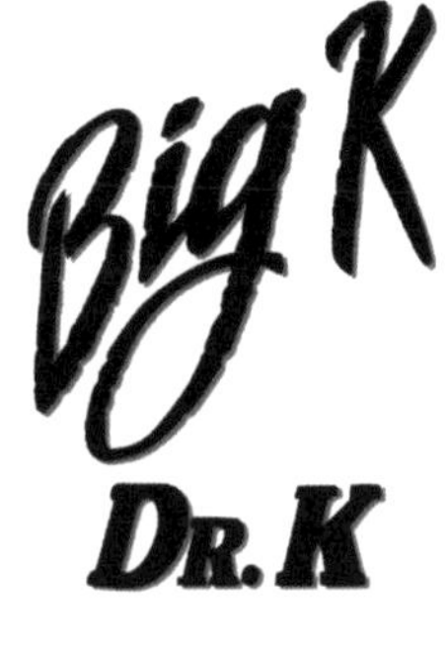

30.

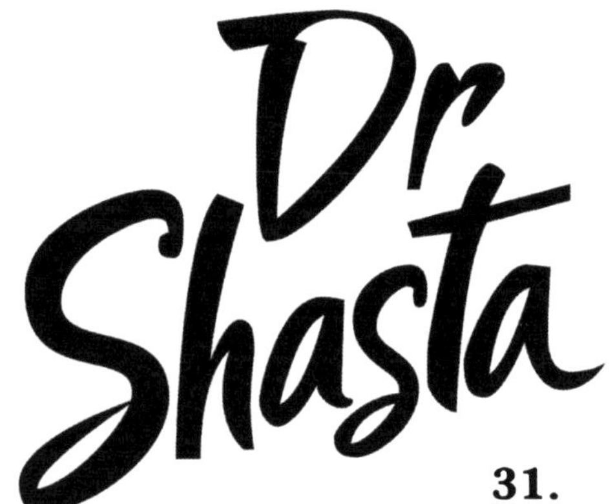

31.

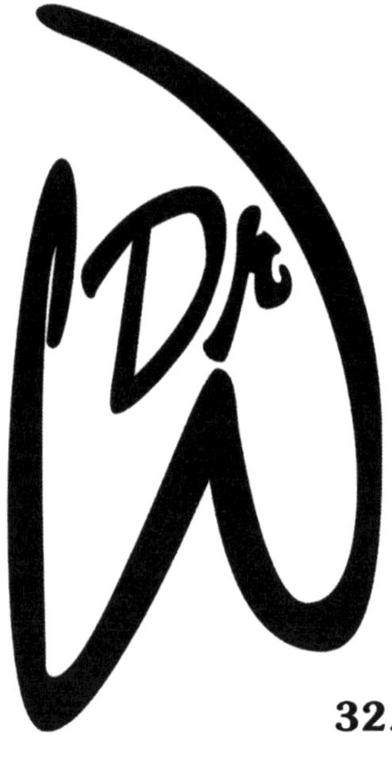

32.

30. Dr. K, mid-2000s. Kroger Company, Cincinnati, Oh. A staple of the author's childhood. **31.** Dr Shasta, 2022. Shasta Beverages, Inc., Hayward, Calif. Introduced in 1990. ‡ **32.** Dr W, date unknown. Wegmans Food Markets, Inc., Rochester, N.Y. ‡. **33.** Dr Lynn, date unknown. Ingles Markets, Inc., Black Mountain, N.C. ‡ **34.** Doctor Cola, 2022. Our Family Foods, a division of SpartanNash, Grand Rapids, Mich. The rare example of the honorific fully spelled out. **35.** Dr. Zing, date unknown. Giant Food, Landover, Md. **36.** Dr. Buzz, date unknown. Western Family Foods, a private label of Save-On-Foods, Langely, B.C., Canada.

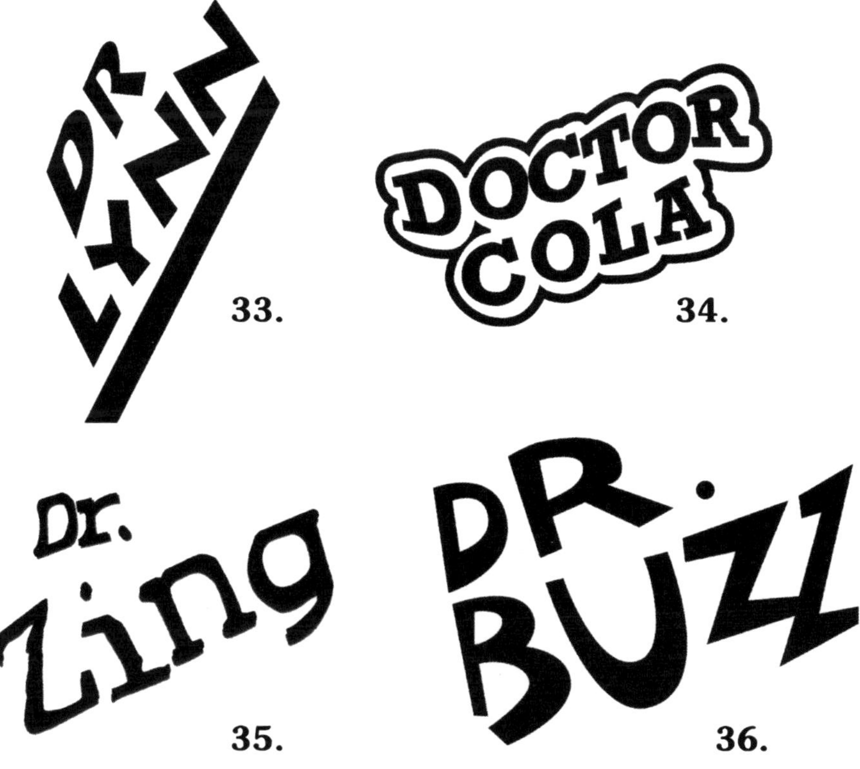

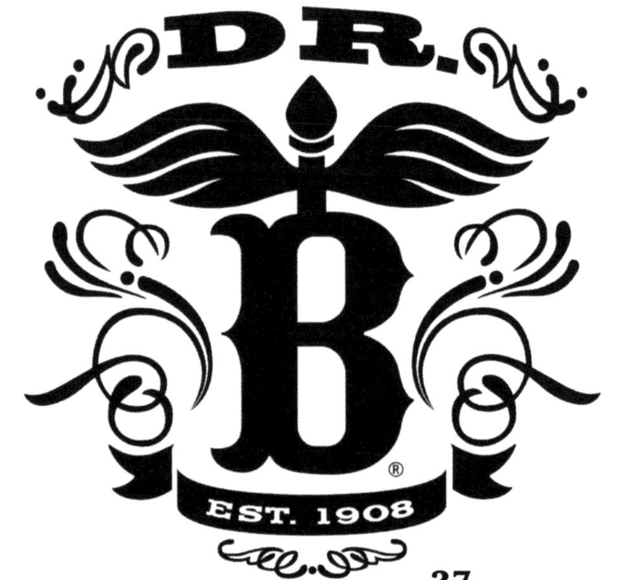

37.

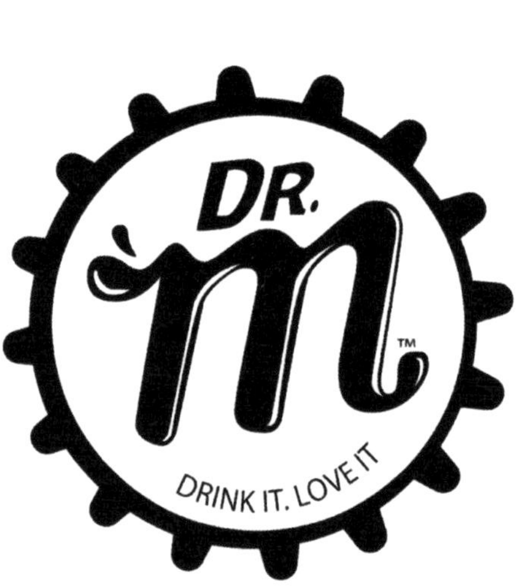

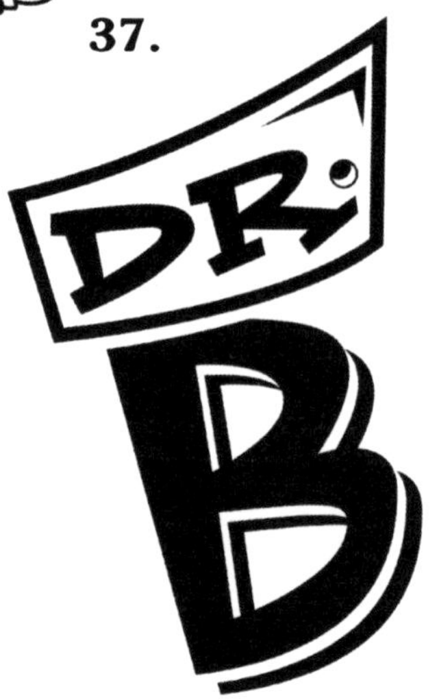

38.

39.

37. Dr. B, 2020. H-E-B Grocery
Company, Houston Tex. A re-
brand emphasizing the "old-timey"
qualities of the Houston-based
supermarket giant's Dr Pepper-de-
rived soda, which takes on extra
resonance in Texas, home of the
original Dr Pepper. This logo is
featured against an outline of Texas
on the packaging. The "est. 1908"
refers most likely to the grocery
chain, not the drink itself. **38.** Dr.
M, 2020. Meiijer, Inc., Greenville, Mich. The updated version of
the "Dr. M" mark in example 14.
39. Dr. B, 2010. H-E-B Grocery
Company, Houston Tex. An earlier
version of the Dr. B mark, typically
"fun" and modern in the style of
the turn of the millennium.

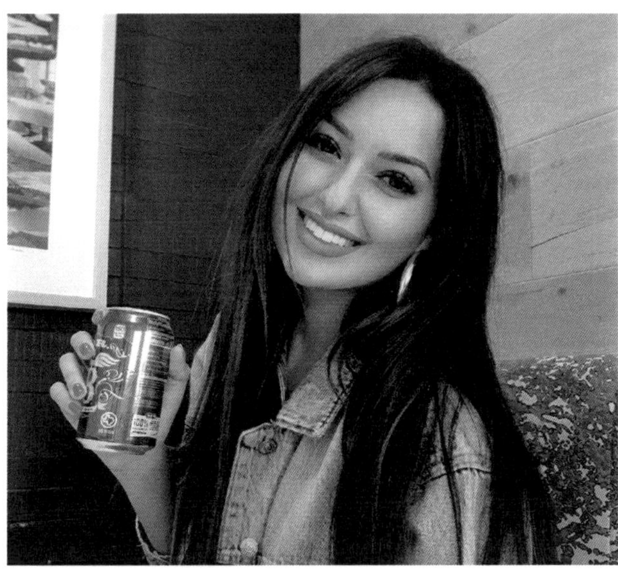

Above: A Houstonian enjoying a 12 oz. can of Dr. B
with the refreshed, Texas-centric packaging. Photo
courtesy Estelle Gaither.

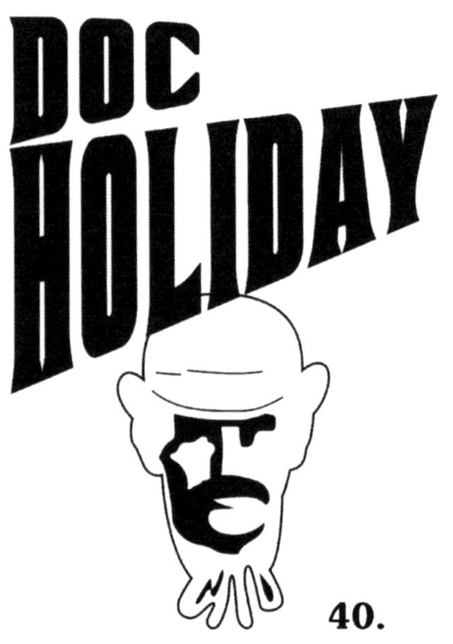

40.

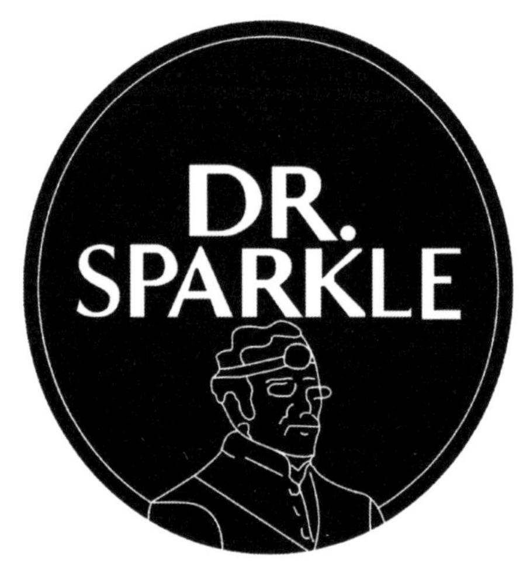

41.

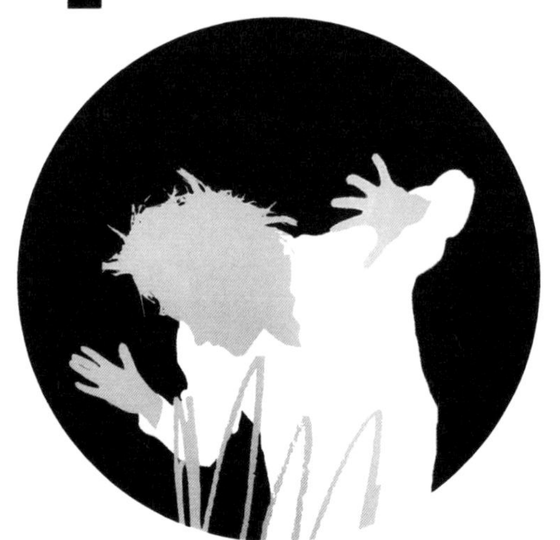

42.

40. Doc Holiday, 2019. Southeastern Bottling Company, Safford, Ariz. Note that "Holiday" is spelled with one "l" to avoid a trademark infringement of other beverage brands already named for the historical Doc Holliday. The three designs on the facing page all feature visual depictions of the fictional doctors for whom the products are named in the branding. **41.** Dr. Sparkle, 2020. Price Chopper Supermarkets, Schenectady, N.Y. Dr. Sparkle appears to be a standard issue 19th century doctor, complete with a head mirror. **42.** Dr. Publix, 2020. Publix Super Markets, Inc., Lakeland, Fla. Dr Publix, in contrast to their colleague Dr. Sparkle, appears to operate in the over-caffeinated, wild-haired tradition of Doc Brown in the *Back to the Future* films. They also appear to be dancing wildly. Were it not for their white lab coat, you might not even recognize Dr. Publix as a medical professional. ‡

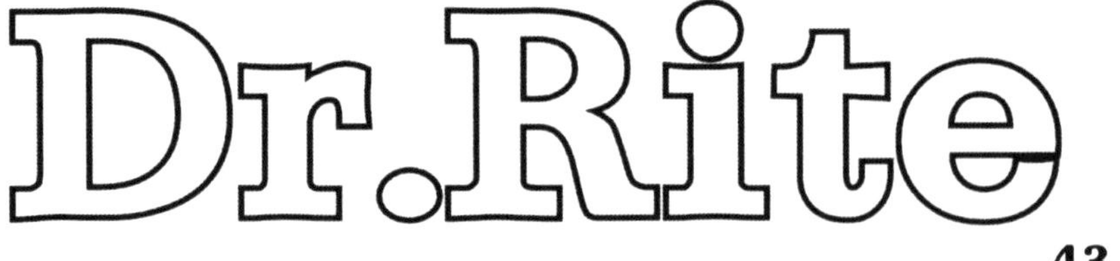

43.

DR. RIFFIC

44.

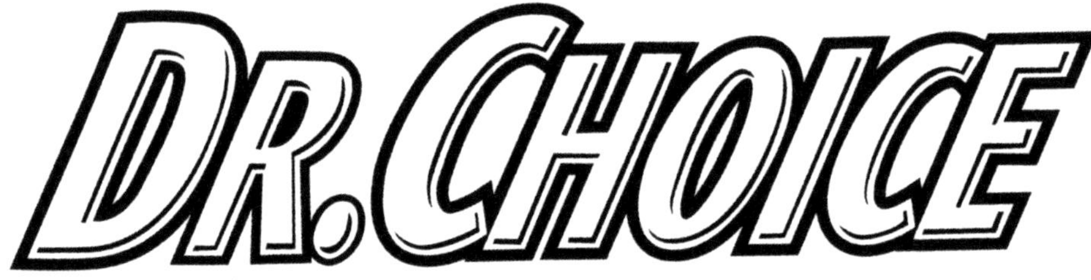

45.

DR. ROCKET

46.

Country Doctor

47.

43. Dr. Rite, date unknown. ShopRite Cooperative, Keasbey, N.J. **44**. Dr. Riffic, early 2000s. Eckerd Pharmacy Corporation, Largo, Fla. **45**. Dr. Choice, 2020. Best Choice Products, Tustin, Calif. **46**. Dr. Rocket, c. 1990s. Kmart, Hoffman Estates, Ill. Another staple of the author's childhood. Dr. Rocket was replaced by Dr. Smart (see 51), representing Kmart's efforts to refresh their private label brand following their bankruptcy. **47**. Country Doctor, mid-2010s. Fareway Stores, Inc., Boone, Iowa. Like some of its fellow doctors, Country Doctor has more recently adopted a more "old-timey" logomark.

48. Dr. Perky, late 2010s. Food Lion, Salisbury, N.C. **49**. Dr. Right, early 2000s. SuperValu, Eden Prairie, MN. Not to be confused with ShopRite's Dr. Rite. **50**. Dr. Smooth, late 2010s. President's Choice / Le Choix du Président, Brampton, Ontario, Canada. **51**. Dr. Smart, late 2010s. Smart Sense, a private label of Kmart, Hoffman Estates, Ill. Dr. Smart replaces their forerunner Dr. Rocket. **52**. The Dr. Soda, early 2010s. Old Time Brands, Wooster, Oh. Not to be confused with the Real Dr. (example 20)

dr.
perky

48.

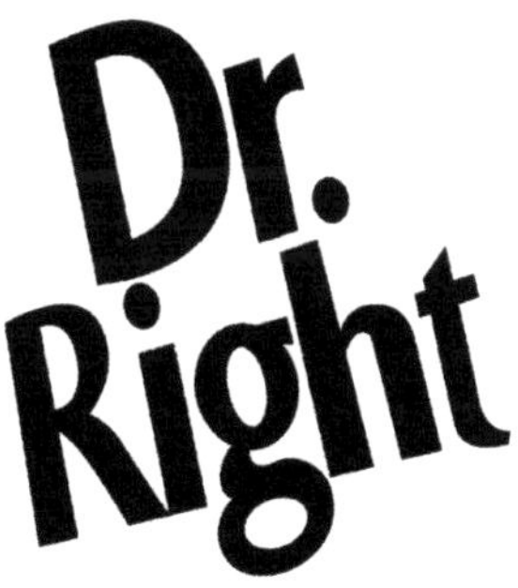

49.

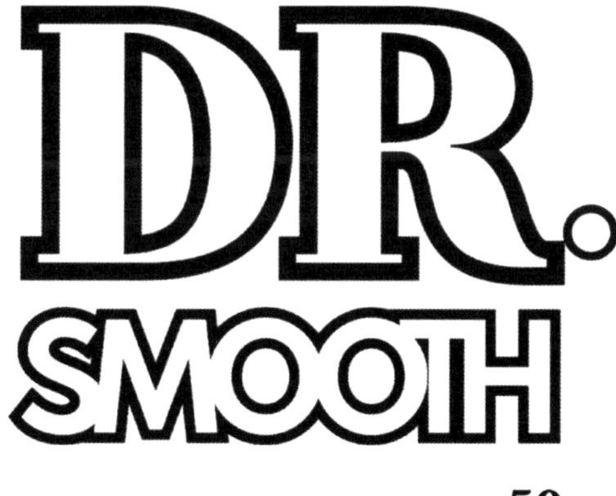

50.

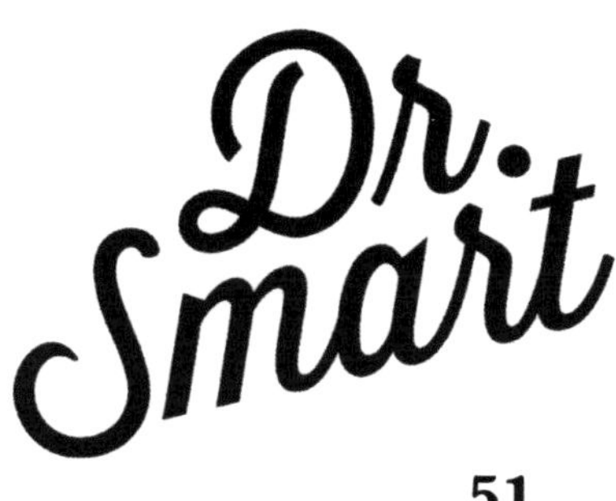

51.

the **Dr.**
SODA

52.

53. Dr. Sparkle, early 2000s. Price Chopper Supermarkets, Schenectady, N.Y. The logomark before the doctor was given a portrait (example 41). **54**. Dr Phizz, 2008. Schnucks Markets, Inc., St. Louis, Mo. ‡ **55**. Dr. Vess, date unknown. Vess Soda, St. Louis, Mo. ‡ **56**. Dr. Shaw's, 2020. Shaw's and Star Market, West Bridgewater, Mass. **57**. Dr. Thunder, early 2020s. Wal-Mart, Bentonville, Ark. **58**. Dr. Flave, late 2010s. Wal-Mart Canada, Mississauga, Ontario, Canada. ‡

53.

54.

55.

56.

57.

58.

Geographic index

United States

Alabama: 21
Arizona: 15, 40
Arkansas: 57
California: 19, 21, 23, 45
Florida: 20, 42, 44
Georgia: 29
Idaho: 17, 26
Illinois: 9, 25, 27, 46, 51
Indiana: 1, 2, 3
Iowa: 47
Maryland: 11, 35
Massachusetts: 56
Michigan: 14, 34, 38
Minnesota: 49

Missouri: 10, 24, 54, 55
New Jersey: 43
New York: 18, 32, 41, 53
North Carolina: 33, 48
Ohio: 30, 52
Oregon: 12
Texas: 16, 28, 37, 39

Canada

British Columbia: 36
Ontario: 50, 58

United Kingdom

Herfordshire: 13

Cover photo and modeling by Yulia Bromley.

Rear back photo by John Margolies, Steele Country Kitchen sign, Route 29, Pensacola, Florida, 1979. John Margolies Roadside America photograph archive (1972-2008), Library of Congress, Prints and Photographs Division.

Printed in Carver County, Minnesota, the traditional and contemporary homelands of the Sisseton and Wahpeton bands of the Dakhóta people. A percentage of Birchwood Palace Industries' annual revenue is contributed to Dakota Wicohan, a Native-led non-profit educational organization located within the Lower Sioux Indian Community that seeks to revitalize the Dakota language and lifeways in Minnesota. Learn more about the organization at dakotawicohan.org.